Breath, Like Water

01 02 03 04 05 25 24 23 22 21

Caitlin Press Inc.
3375 Ponderosa Way
Qualicum Beach, BC
www.caitlin-press.com

Text design by Vici Johnstone
Cover design by Sarah Corsie
Cover images derived from "Development" by Natasha Harvey
Printed in Canada

Caitlin Press Inc. acknowledges financial support from the Government of Canada and the Canada Council for the Arts, and the Province of British Columbia through the British Columbia Arts Council and the Book Publisher's Tax Credit.

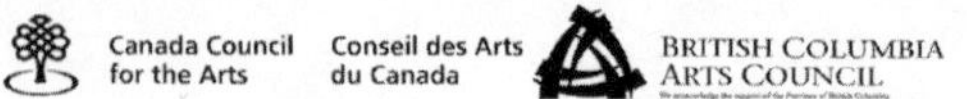

Funded by the Government of Canada | Canada

Library and Archives Canada Cataloguing in Publication
Breath, like water : an anticolonial romance / Norah Bowman.
Bowman, Norah, author.

Poems.

Canadiana 20210215607 | ISBN 9781773860657 (softcover)
LCC PS8603.O97665 B74 2021 | DDC C811/.6—dc23

Breath, Like Water

An Anticolonial Romance

NORAH BOWMAN

Caitlin Press 2021

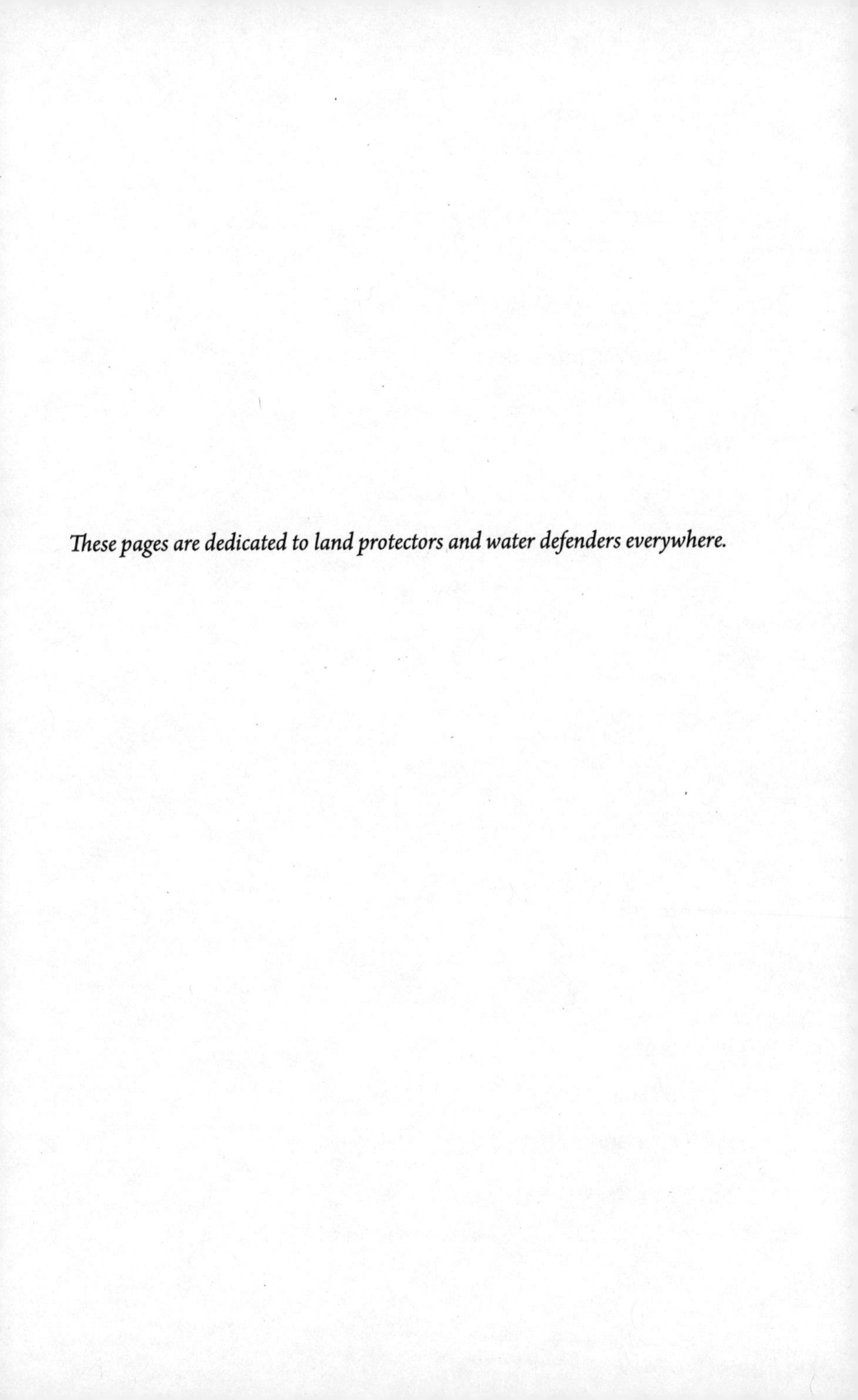

These pages are dedicated to land protectors and water defenders everywhere.

Contents

Another Way to Say I Love Mountain

Women lacing their boots and walking,

weary and spiteful, away from children and men.

Women who leave a note *Gone for a walk.*

Women who leave the doors unlocked, dishes dirty, men unsoothed.

Women who wake before dawn.

Look, Mountain does not need me.

Mountain needs pinecone-bursting fires, seed spreading floods, nut-cracking birds, larva-scraping bears, fish-feeding flies, vole-warming snows, stone-breaking mudslides.

Look, my grandmother walked Mountain too. As she walked she would tear a twig from a pine branch, swing that twig like a taser, poke and complain.

My grandmother and I walked Okanagan Mountain together. She, following trails, scrabbling in the soft earth with her long branch. Me, looping behind, ahead, around, off the trail, on the trail, so young and unbitter, imagining cities. My grandmother had an eye for the lichen and moss growing on the forest floor and would sometimes fall to her knees, look close to a decaying fallen tree. I wish I'd listened when she told me about pixie cup lichen, freckle pelt lichen, step moss. She didn't pick them, but would kneel there, telling me the qualities of each small forest at our feet. I had no patience for the scale of lichen and moss.

Look, my Irish English great grandmother hated mountains, especially every mountain in these unceded Indigenous territories. She was born to the soft green of Munster hills and travelled to England as a nurse in 1917. I know she loved Percy Bysshe Shelley and Lord George Byron; my grandmother showed me the very chapter of poetry my great grandmother had carried to Canada and filled with lonely annotations. She must have dreamt of a sailboat, an officer, serge, a castle. Instead she fucked an injured Canadian soldier in Devon, and her English father forced her to marry him and take herself and her embryos to Winnipeg. My great grandmother did not ever forgive Canada for forcing her to leave Ireland, England, and poetry. Moving to warm Vancouver barely lightened her resentment.

Look, I come from a line of angry women.

I am not in love with mountains, or rivers, or poetry.

I am in love with Mountain.

Bang
Bang

When Priest bootsteps bang like bullets into soil,

bootsole flattens
coiled lichen arms,
shatters all grace in
ponderosa pine needles.

The walking man has
no time for
lichen
or
pines.

Blistered face
rudded hair
his sweat streams
a great fear
and
a great anger.

This priest and his men take no time to love Mountain.

They walk Mountain as though she is no

more than a
cursed scab

between glory and gold.

Priest

sings dirty prayers to saskatoon berries
forgives no snake across his path
crushes coral flowered cacti
along Mountain's pass.

Thus fell the first angry white steps on Mountain.

On unceded Syilx territory,

traditional land of the Okanagan People,

Okanagan Mountain

still hums

alive of granite,

berries,

gold,

water,

Snake.

An Anticolonial Romance

Okanagan Mountain's

          animal people

and

          insect people

burrow resistance

through

          fire and flood.

Mountain reads the intent of every

footstep   on the   soil,

and like a   thawing river

     cannot   help but breathe

a welcome to all warm life.

Oblivious to Mountain's

righteous welcome, the poisonous invader's feet

walked on   and

     walked   off

mountain.

Still, Mountain broke

horseshoes, cosseted

rattlesnakes, burned

faces.

So Priest and

his men cut a long, slow trail around

Mountain's softer eastern slopes.

Settlers brought their

own workers, housed them

barely.

Governors transported

prisoners to

work the fruit orchards,

bankers borrowed on

slavery loans

to mortgage the

lakefront villas.

Even today, antebellum

verandahs

cup the villas all

along lakeside sands,

like fragile wooden pastries.

The houses

cars and
social workers

churches and
teachers

police and
wineries

legislators and
metal scrappers

farmers and
bankers

orchards and
miners

drinkers and
schools

remittance men and
wives.

Syilx people do not cede

the land. LAND BACK

Neither Mountain nor valley,

neither lake nor river, neither fish nor berry. LAND BACK

Syilx stories are Okanagan people stories to tell—not mine— LAND BACK

and Syilx stories and being LAND BACK

have lived and told and listened here LAND BACK

for time beyond time. LAND BACK

It is my intent to return Mountain and Lake LAND BACK

all the land LAND BACK

animal people LAND BACK

bird people LAND BACK

fish people LAND BACK

insect people to Syilx stories. LAND BACK

I do not tell Syilx stories. I am not Syilx. LAND BACK

What I can tell today is a story of Priest's people,

the settlers,

and their

burning.

When Mountain Held Ocean

When, in what time, did Mountain hold Ocean?

Okanagan Mountain held Ocean held Okanagan Mountain

mountains ago

many oceans ago.

Breathing of quartz granite iron ore gold through sky-seeing ocean eyes.

Mountain measured themself away from Ocean an ellipsis ago.

Mountain is a colonized name:

it is making a nation-state out of a people,

a husband out of a lover.

Maps mark Mountain as an elevation of stone, as if by height alone Mountain lives. What a sham! What a wrong!

Mountain is a vast swelling in the soil, a lift of desire from core to ozone.
Mountain sings sorrow from afar.
Mountain grieves the death of a warrior lover after only nine moons of love.
Mountain mosses the burial of childhood.
Mountain architects every human memory of nighttime.

Mountain holds lakes and rivers
exhales rains and clouds
reaches roots through hooves
flakes scales
hemafuses uteruses.

On a June day I first walk all the way up Mountain, the 10 km of high dry trail, ascending one kilometre to a tiny glacial lake folded into the mountaintop.

Most of Mountain's ponderosa pines burned in a week-long fire in 2003.
Aside from a brief glade of untouched ponderosa pines at the lower slopes, the walk is scorching hot, shadeless.

I Walk All the Way up Mountain

That first walk up Mountain burns my skin and dries my eyes. The fire of 2003 burned all but one small grove of ponderosa pines. I ascend the western slope, blazing in afternoon heat.

> Hot as my great grandmother's eternal hatred of
> ships and men.

My mind map and paper map show that there is a tiny lake, Divide Lake, at the peak of Okanagan Mountain, a bleed of blue between two narrow cliffs. Paper map shows a tiny campsite at Divide Lake. I am carrying overnight supplies to stay my first night with Okanagan Mountain, the mountain whom I do not yet love. My bootsteps are tentative, my eyes are slow, the walk is long but the path is wide and clear.

> As my great grandmother's eternal hot hatred of
> men and ships.

After the five hour walk I arrive at Divide Lake. I take off my heavy pack and feel remarkably *well.*
Feet and fingers
feel intimate with warm
humming Mountain.

> My great grandmother's hot eternal hatred of
> men and ships.

When I arrive, anywhere, when I arrive after a journey—sweating five hours up a mountain, or sitting fourteen hours in planes and cars—when I arrive at a place, I like to lay down on my back, close my eyes, and listen to the ground.

> Hot hatred of ships and men, my great grandmother,
> eternal.

Listen to Ground

Hear the hiss of dead pine needles pressed to my damp skull.
And little pine beetle a legged grain of rice, scurrying.
In truth I am neither psychic nor indigenous to this land so
the stories are not speaking from the aquifer into my mind.
I hear   heart sailing.
I hear   eyelashes curtaining.
I hear   my own life folding,
and particles hard softs layer, colonial soil, under my old body.

Laying Down and Sleeping

So in this way I lay down with Okanagan Mountain for the first time, settling cool in the shade of Engelmann spruce. They stand as if tired by their own green bodies, boughs spreading groundwards. On the mountaintop, winds parent spruce trees into improbable many-armed shapes. Some lean east for years, then grow west, then stop growing taller and only spread wider, lower, with ragged density. Some grow always to the south, leaning to warmth.

I lay among the Spruce people,
at the windy mountaintop.

And I feel the sweetness of the backs of my burning calves pressing on cool pebbles. Sweat dries and cools along my neck. A sensation of a fine mud of sweat and soil shivers my vertebrae.

The songs of bird people here trilling the high blue sky of mountain peak.

At the windy mountaintop,
I lay among the Spruce people.

Wind crashes and catches in spruce boughs, pushing against dense short needles.

I let my wrists relax on scattered pine needles and grey stony soil. My hair will be speckled with dirt and my hands indented by pebbles and twigs. In this knowing and feeling, listening and cooling, I move from consciousness of walker to consciousness of rester. Not quite asleep, on my way to sleep, the hypnagogic state of being awake, asleep, on a mountain, in the summer air.

Among the Spruce people,
laying at the mountaintop.

A half dream, a half waking, orchestra of fish jumping and wind pushing, my sweat cooling shiver becoming a fine body quake, bird calls bleating from bird-people hearts. The dreamspace is mountain berries, mountain trees, mountain shape, *mountain mountain mountain.*

Spruce people, among laying
at the mountaintop.

Another Time I Walk to Divide Lake on Okanagan Mountain

Another time, I walk to Divide Lake and back to the city in one day.
I walk this after leaving a human lover, softly closing a Kelowna City door to his face.

My lover smelled like a cedar grove after rain.

He
kissing me like drinking water from a cold creek.
He
as big and warm as a black bear, as gentle as a jackrabbit.
He
holding me in the air and making love to me like that, my eyes aloft.

A bricklayer,
his hands had grown into massive softened paws,
his arms swollen as spring freshet.

But his mind went hypnagogic when it should have been awake.

When his huge body would
hurt
after days of long labour,
his mind

would melt a little around the edges.

After sex I felt ashamed to see his frightened eyes.

Like walking out of a burning forest,
I left him but looked back again.

Bears

That time, walking off my grief at leaving my bear lover, I was not attentive to Mountain's snowy peak. In this heedless state I took the mountain trail too early in the season, dressed in valley shorts and soft spring shoes. As I began my walk the sun was bright and warm.

At 6 km, that is, two thirds up Mountain, the muddy trail iced over. By 6.5 I was walking through snow, about 10 cm, the depth of a hand. The snow was yellowed with a heavy old crust, and under the crust, pockets of collapsed snow hid holes the size of badgers, and under those holes, half-iced slush.

By 7 km up Mountain, I was walking through 60 cm, each step breaking the crust, each step sliding through old snow to slush.

By 7.5 km up Mountain, my bare thighs landed in the pockets of cold air and crust with each step, and my feet were wet through and frozen.

As I stepped through the cold crust, my calves scraped on the icy edges, bleeding bright specks onto the white trail.

But I kept walking—why turn back now? So close. So close to the peak, to the little lake hidden at the top.

At the peak, the snow lay about in massive jagged drifts, branches of burned trees and tops of young spruce trees jutting out. Few birds sang, and the lake was frozen over grey and green.
I guessed the bears and snakes were sleeping under fallen-pine caverns.

I did not lay down and listen to Mountain. I turned around and walked back down.

Bear Forest

"Black bears are forest bears, but they prefer forests with holes in them...
those where the tree canopy is sparse or patchy enough that sunlight can reach
the forest floor."

As the plane slid from the sky it tore

an uneven
swath through ponderosa pines,
landing broken-hulled in
winter forest.

Making airplane bear forest.

Fire makes bear forest.

In the coal dust of afterfires,
green needled pines live among
sootfields,
blackened snags.

"No longer obscured by tree foliage, the soil soon erupts with greenery, and
over the next several years ants and other insects invade the wood of the dead
trees.... [O]ur twentieth-century success at putting out forest fires has result-
ed in the gradual deterioration of bear habitat in many years."

In 2003, a week-long wildfire
burned most of
Mountain's dense
ponderosa pines and cottonwood
forests.

Fire flew from burning

trees to burning

218 houses at the

bottom of

Mountain.

In the first years after the fire, fireweed covers the burned earth.

Fireweed grows in thick patches,
almost like a lawn, spackled with

flowers,
purpling shamelessly on the
carbon
rich soil.

In time, with a decade or more of universe-making,

ponderosa pine,

red willow,

cottonwood

saplings break through the glassy crust that forms on burned soil,
jubilant on

nitrogen and coal,

released by fire,

ready for bear people and
deer people.

Even now, decades after the fire, blanched and blackened trunks and branches crosshatch most of the mountain. Each spring, old coal mingles with wildflowers. Bear roams with leisure, pulling beetles, mice, pinecones, fireweed roots from this delicate and fecund fabric.

Most of Mountain's dry cliffs and

dark damp valleys remain

unwelcoming to car and condominium.

Before the Fire

Before the 2003 wildfire, most settler-colonial citizens of Kelowna could not name Mountain if asked. They saw Mountain only when her fire towered above the city for two hot weeks. They saw Mountain only when her burning moved into those little suburbs. Only then did Mountain aflame become a person for the city.

The settlers storied Mountain as masqueraded with a villainous fire, as if it were Mountain who was a visitor intent on conquest. As if she became her own house-hungry fire.

Let me say, that to love Mountain is to love fire.
To love Mountain is to swallow coal.
Mountain love sees freshet love.
Mountain love learns seedling love.

You who are fearful of fire,
your love fails
like cash over flame.

In the decades since the fire, City of Kelowna people
forget Mountain
again.

Fire Paper Body

"This makes the thing we are looking at very different and this makes what those who describe it make of it, it makes a composition, it confuses, it shows, it is, it looks, it likes it as it is, and this makes what is seen as it is seen."
—Gertrude Stein

Look, perhaps I love Mountain

because

burned body

recognizes

burned body.

And love is a body fingering its scar-mirror.

make a composition

Let me say that while I have thus always lived with
scalpel-marked trachea,
puzzle-fleshed body
and pebbled skin-graft thighs,
and while I have come to expect other human people to
blush at my scars,
I am nevertheless moved to tears when
a human person touches me
with kindness
rather than abhorrence.

it confuses

Look, perhaps I love Mountain

it shows
it looks

because the

old rippled burns on my body

recognize the

old rippled burns on Mountain's body.

what is seen
as it is seen

Ticks

I am not the first
spring walker
in love
with a mountain.

First woman in love with a mountain?
No.
First woman in love with *this* mountain?
Maybe.
First white walker in love with Mountain since the big fire?
Yes. I must be.

Though every lover believes she is the only.

Spring this year is dry - Mountain may be on fire by summer.
And I am wary of ticks.

In May and June the Tick people crawl fecund, hungry.

When I walk Mountain in May and June I can not
pause
to sit on the trail.

If I were to set my pack on the trail for a moment,
a Tick person would
leap
onto the straps, hike
towards my body. I touch my feet to the
trail
lightly,
quickly.

By and Leaps

Tick person clings to a blade of grass

swaying with bloodhungry vertigo   until

a proper Uexküllian mammal   brushes by   and

Tick   leaps.

Leap (what is leap)
leap like a fly with
oval body flattened as
a kite with legs peeled
back like rocket
wings / unto the
heady fog of carbon
dioxide and ammo-
nia / until mammal
heat opens a window
and Tick tenders
her body forward in
starving flight

and brushes   by
Tick leaps

oh she comes to hold
hirsute body with
ever clenching tiny
claws and / climb
Tick climbs she
climbs towards the
hot sun of carbon
dioxide emissions /
towards the hottest
orbit on the walking
blood / towards the
thickest warmest
red-richest place and
finally

brushes by
Tick leaps and

can release salivating
mouth onto such
thin brainskin / Tick
is gentle her mouth
releases the tenderest
analgesic as her body
burrows headfirst
into mammalblood /
the engorgement of
(tongue wet) (desire
yields) (completion)

Tick
brushes by and
leaps

knowing blood / she
swells she darkens
she hardens and /
falls from mammal
/ stumbles for soil
and for egg laying
(oviparian release
/ oviparous / child
production / concep-
tion).

Woodworker

This dry year I have fallen in love with Karol, a carpenter who builds staircases in mansions along Mountain's lower slopes. He likes to build unusual structures, taking on what other carpenters reject as finicky. Little pieces of wood, cut in circles and triangles, fitted together tightly, tapped with tool only once. Wide staircases tapering from marble entrances, showy spiral staircases hanging over sunken living rooms, narrow steps hugging fireplaces, balconies, attics. He is modest about his unusual skill, says to me, "I'm just a guy with a hammer," and he is, and I love him.

He calls me at lunch every day, listens easily when I detail the life cycle of a tick, the difficulties of identifying spruce at high elevations.

He minds just a little when I am vacant, my eyes away, heart on Mountain.

Makes love to me with kindness, slowly, testing his grip on my thigh a little more each time, and only after a year does he press me hard to enough to leave a soft thumbprint on my hip.

Not a Bear person so much as a Human person.

I don't hold it against Karol that he builds the houses into the mountainside; I have a Marxist analysis of labour so I resent the speculators, the owners, the bankers, but not the guy with a hammer.

Golden Mile Trail

Autumn. I walk Okanagan Mountain's Golden Mile Trail, a 1.1 km walk from the road, first along a steep ridge, right side of my face towards the lake, left side towards the trees. Then I follow west, some kilometres through standing ponderosas only partly burned, coal black at the bottom but green and weighty with needles far above the reach of fire. Wet boulders crest out of the soil, their surfaces blue and orange and grey. Some stones are smooth and some jagged. A faux sand of crushed pine needles reddens in slim stone crevasses, held in place with tiny lichens and mosses.

The trail turns through an aspen grove, bright green and yellow coin shaped leaves turning and glittering, soft white trunks growing close. When a wind lifts the leaves there is a gentle clattering at my face. I stop and place my palms on an aspen trunk, and when I lift a hand I am dusted with a soft grey powder. Aspen's thin bark is cool, even on a hot day. Aspen bark's vulnerability has always terrified me, as if with one misplaced kick a single deer could tear at Aspen's body. I lift my hands away and continue walking through the grove. The soil is damp, soft, spongy with golden aspen-leaf hummus. A single mountain creek pools at Aspen's rhizome roots. It is a small grove and in minutes I return to rocky pine forest.

As always on Mountain, as I walk I look from side to side, listening for rustling, for breathing. I attend to rocks tumbling from the small cliffs that rise out of Mountain. Fall is Bear person, Cougar person, and Snake person hungry season. Saskatoon berries are wizened, huckleberries and thimbleberries have fallen, and tender spring roots are now hard and dry; Mountain's animal people need any last calories before snow comes.

But I don't quite know what Bear people eat in the fall, except fish from a creek, and the creeks filled with spawning fish are at least 20 km from this west slope of Mountain. So why would Bear be here at all? I should ask a biologist. I would think Bear person is not here, except that on the trail I come across their steaming fresh scat, big and black and filled with fibrous matter. Not berry seeds. Not fish bones. What are you eating, Bear person?

Later I ask Syilx Okanagan person Frank Marchand, my friend Bill Cohen's cousin, why I would find fresh bear scat on a dry autumn mountain. Frank said, "Bear people are passing through, on their way to a creek. Crossing territory."

As for Cougar people, they don't hibernate, so Cougar is always walking, looking for rabbits, deer, mice, cats, dogs, humans. Anything that demands fewer calories than its flesh provides; I remind myself to appear big and full of fight, not worth the attack.

I walk with joy. Mountain in the fall is bright, the light falls clear but gentle, in the rare groves of cottonwood and aspen the leaves shift from green to yellow to orange, mosses glow on the wet rocks, the sky is cloudless, the sun doesn't burn my neck, and everything smells wet and clean. Ticks are unhungry, Mountain is always closed to human hunters, and I like being on Mountain during the fall.

On this day, once I walk 3 km I am in the quiet burned land. The trail is well worn and wide but I don't see any human or animal people. All I see and hear is Mountain. A few trees remain standing, russet dark ponderosa trunks like brush marks against a grey and green terrain. Mostly the land is thick with fallen half-burned pines, their bark long since torn or fallen off. In my first visits to Mountain I saw the dead pines as fallen bodies, as if from a war. But now I see the openness between them hugged by thick berry bushes, willow bushes, grasses. In this fire-scraped landscape I can see very far, I can see across a valley, across a small peak, across another valley, and I scan for movement, always.

Scanning for Bear people or Squirrel people or Deer people, I see none. Bird people, but not many. A Snake person, but not clearly. If not for the Mushrooms and Lichen and Moss people I would be alone.

Arriving at a flat blueish boulder, I rest, laying down on stone. I feel the small smooth ridges—mountains of another scale—under my hips. I finger the fragile cups and curls of moss and lichen who have found a whisper of nutrient and water in which to grow. A watery green moss dampens the back of my neck. In my breath a blue metallic taste of rocky soil, cold on my lungs. Mountain's air a medicine along my scarred trachea.

Walking back I am quicker, less mindful of Bear people and Cougar people, as if they know I am walking away from the mountain now, so they will let me pass.

City

What the
City of Kelowna feels like is that nothing
that is alive
moves.

Dry winds blow dead dollars into alley corners, old clothes clog creeks. Some of our politicians don't believe in anthropogenic climate change. Don't *believe,* as if our burning mountains, car-enjambed roads, struggling Salmon people, disappearing Turtle people are a matter of belief.

Gated community fence
Gated communiteeeee fences
Gated community fensssssss

And while the roads were built by forced labour, and the fruit trees have been pruned and polished by interned labour hands, by migrant labour hands, by underpaid workers, and the hospital cleaned and kept by generations of workers kept away from beaches and verandahs, and the land here the creeks here the beaches here are the home of Syilx people living with Deer people, Bear people, Salmon people, Cactus people, Ponderosa Pine people, it is now

Pandosy Street
Lakeshore Road
Magic Estates
Wilden Estates
Missionview Estates
Appleridge Road
Crawford Road
Richter Street

every softpaved road pressing away the animal people the human people the tree people the insect people who have populated and would still populate the space of this valley
Spread
Out
Below
Mountain
Between
Lake
And
Mountain.

Excepting, the space of heaving light and scar-open humanity,
the Tent City of human

people experiencing homelessness experiencing
verandahlessness experiencing cashlessness
experiencing carelessness experiencing
shoelessness experiencing whitelessness
experiencing hatlessness experiencing
windowlessness experiencing

Here the human people are breathing in the cold and hot air, living alongside the butterfly people, mouse people, fly people, raccoon people, rat people. Many Indigenous human people camp here, unwelcome by those goldening voices of cash & steel.

In a cross section, Tent City is structured thus

Silt soil
Gravel
Cement
Polyester tent
Torn duvet
Torn duvet
Plaid sleeping bag
Human person
Cotton shirt
Polyester jacket
Plaid sleeping bag
Torn duvet
Polyester tent
Sky
Human police people
Baton
Gun
Human police people
Sky

Lake

LAND BACK WATER BACK LAND BACK WATER BACK LAND BACK WATER BACK
LAND BACK WATER BACK LAND BACK WATER BACK LAND BACK WATER BACK

In winter, often, when I can't visit the mountain, when the city and I hustle all day and all night, and no daylight hours are left for walking to Okanagan Mountain, I soothe-balm my heart with a walk to Okanagan Lake. Lake doesn't freeze anymore in the winter.

LAND BACK WATER BACK LAND BACK WATER BACK LAND BACK WATER BACK
LAND BACK WATER BACK LAND BACK WATER BACK LAND BACK WATER BACK

Lake wends from the base of Okanagan Mountain, along the rancid heritage villas, along beaches, along parks, along human settlement, past the City of Kelowna. So I approach her unfrozen shores from colonial land-steal settlement, walk along park-thieved lands and lawns.

LAND BACK WATER BACK LAND BACK WATER BACK LAND BACK WATER BACK
LAND BACK WATER BACK LAND BACK WATER BACK LAND BACK WATER BACK

I hold my hand in Lake's winter water until my skin pinks, until my skin blues. Mountain streams, melted mountain snows, heavy spring and fall rains compose the lake. How long do I need to keep my hand in the lake until my bones welcome Mountain's water? I want my hand to breathe in through fingernail, knuckle, wrist. I ask my blood to accept the melted mountain water. I will my hand permeable.

LAND BACK WATER BACK LAND BACK WATER BACK LAND BACK WATER BACK
LAND BACK WATER BACK LAND BACK WATER BACK LAND BACK WATER BACK

Witch's Butter

Most days I circulate through the city,
dodging human faces I fear, looking away
with anxiety and sadness from human faces
I don't fear. I close my eyes and recall
my recent adoration I met on Mountain,
a particular fallen pine, fire-blackened at
one end, soft brown moldering at another
end, and a glistening orange witch's butter
spackling all along its length, looking for all
the world like a branch spread with neon
cheese, but as tender and moist, as alive
and hungry as I.

Birth and Danger

"When a loved one is suffering a lot, he or she doesn't have enough energy to embrace you and help you to suffer less. So it's natural that you become disappointed. You think that the other person's presence is no longer helpful to you. You may even wonder if you love this person anymore."
—Thich Nhat Hanh, *How to Love*

There were at least 12,000 Okanagan human
people living throughout Okanagan Syilx territory
before settler-colonial plagues and violences.

A glacier lobe melted very slowly, an oceanic lake forming around a core of stagnant ice. As the ice dam was breached and water spilled through valleys, the level of glacial lake began to drop. The core melted over millennia. A series of silt bluffs and eroded scarps formed as the ice lake drained. Thousands of summers and thousands of winters passed, and as the core finally melted completely, a depression was left. Under the hard soil a glacial body became buried, and when it melted, the soil yielded and the ice melted to form Okanagan Lake. Rock hills, dry benches, and patchy veneer of moraine rock birth Okanagan Mountain.

Mountain rises to the Lake's east, remembering glacial water's world.

Before settler-colonial plagues and violences,
there were at least 12,000 Okanagan human
people living throughout Okanagan Syilx territory.

Mountain protects Okanagan human people pictographs. Spiritual visions, hunting, Deer people, Goat people, Horse people images on Mountain. Some of these paintings on Mountain are at least 2,000 years old.

"... their locations are closely guarded secrets to protect against vandalism."

let's not say vandals.
vandals are
heroes of the night
crushers of capitalism
bread and cheese liberators.

no no no no no no no no
no no no no no no no no
no no no no no no no no
no no no no no no no no
no no no no no no no no
no no no no no noo oo nn
no no no no no no no no
no nn no no no no nn oo
no no no no oo nn
no oo no nn no no no no
no no
no no no no no no no no
no no no no no no no no
no no no no no no no no
no no no no no no no no
no no no no no no no no
no no no no no noo oo nn
no no no no no no no no
no nn no no no no nn oo
no no no no oo nn
no oo no nn no no no no
no no
no no no no no no no no
no no no no no no no no
no no no no no no no no
no no no no no no no no
no no no no no no no no
no no no no no noo oo nn
no no no no no no no no
no nn no no no no nn oo
no no no no oo nn
no oo no nn no no
no no no no

a destruction of Mountain Okanagan pictographs is genocide.
to scrape away a pictograph is to shave love from the land.
stealing pictographs from Mountain peels a living being.

Mountain Protects.

These Experiential Entities

Winter walk on Mountain. Dense icy fog wraps mountain from treetops to sky. From my feet trees rise clearly, but slide away into the fog.

This winter path is damp, blue snow on the trail, and each footprint presses the snow to grey, so that every passing Deer person, Dog person, human person, leaves a blurred intaglio.

The children call my cellphone three times while I am walking.
I tell them to apply cold compresses to bruises, to take fruit and meat for hunger, to rest in a dark room for headaches, to embrace one another when sad. Of course, if I don't answer the phone they would find these remedies themselves. Still, I love these small human people, so I answer their calls.

Mountain answers me every time I call. At my every walk along the granite boulders and flooding creeks, my every step on the squeaking snow, my pains and sorrows are perceived by mountain.

Idealist panpsychism is the view that "the universe is composed of ... experiential entities, and of nothing else. These experiential entities can both perceive one another and be perceived."

These experiential beings, as Ellis calls them, have both an "experiential existence and [an] empirical existence."

The being experiences its own existence, and it interferes with the experiences of other beings enough that the interferences can be measured.

These interferences are measured as grammar, time, colour, heat, remember, crackle, fog, love, answer, rule, gate, metre, wind, call, sweat, salt, weep, grip, forget, conjunction, final.

Ellis and other panpsychists are philosopher physicists, accepting the outer limits of the potentialities of quantum physics to explain existence.

When I say *people*, I mean *experiential being.*

Experiential Beings

City of bright heart / fascists hate cities / fascists idealize life in the country
As if farmhouses
hide fewer horrors than the villas in cities.

In Kelowna, Tent City develops, spreads men and laughter one block east one block west another block south, cigarettes and sandwiches everywhere.

Newspapers and police call Tent City a

Fire
Hazard. Because, the police remind:

Polyester tent +
Oxygen =
Fire.

Police come, 19:18, Thursday, in December. The order:

Roll tents!
Fold blankets!
Get items into carts!
Move off!!

A Recent History of Some Relocated Human People

1.8 kilometres northeast of Lake Okanagan
1.4 kilometres from banks schools gyms bars villas churches

The Mayor of the City authorizes

A security firm fences
A space comprises

a field a
small
snow-brightened
field

Daily at 19:00 the small field's fence folds open
and the human people recently evicted from Leon Avenue rebuild
that night's Tent City:

Glacial till
Soil substrate
Green Cross grass
Snow
Polyester tent
Torn duvet
Torn duvet
Plaid sleeping bag
Human person
Cotton shirt
Polyester jacket
Plaid sleeping bag
Torn duvet
Polyester tent
Snow
Sky
Human guard people hired by city
Baton
Human guard people hired by city
Sky

At 7:00 every morning from
sky to snow, police people
order the human people
recently relocated
from Leon Avenue to
dismantle Tent City.

Between 19:00 and 7:00, human people stand together, human people bring hot food, cold water, and medicine. Some heart-moist human people answer the calls of the human people sleeping behind the fence. The security guard humans fight with the heart-moist humans answering the calls. The humans sleeping in the tents tell stories of having, not having, loving, not loving, needing, not needing, and the humans answering the calls tell the same stories. One night a human person in one tent grows very cold, dies. His tent becomes a small temple, yellow tape do not do not do not cross police do not and human objects arranged around, and people take away his tent, and the earth and pressed cold grass becomes a space where the sadness seeps into the soil, into the glacial till, into the water, into the lake, into the sky, back to Mountain.

Answer

Could Mountain answer the call of this city?
This city of cold and stories and dying?

How soon, Mountain receives snow that

falls with the sorrows of a human person

passing in a tent? His last warm breath

less than fifty metres from houses humming

of

spare rooms,

heated garages,

second fridges.

Snow

Large snowflakes, whole bundles of snow
really, come all night. In the morning,
in the dark cold of the north face I strap on my
snowshoes and turn south towards Mountain peak.
My feet toss mazarine snow behind,
aloft of each iced step.

High above the trail, Mule Deer person stands on a ridge.
Mule Deer's silhouette cuts a staccato shape from burned
forest.

Her body brings slight warmth to steel grey sky.

Still, she is so slender, so like the blackened tree trunks
that I scan the ridge,
see Mule Deer person,
look again and
do not see her,
look once more
and do see her.

Slight warmth to steel grey sky, her body.

What camouflage is this,
that Mule Deer person stands exactly
as the carcasses
of tree persons?

To steel grey sky her body brings slight warmth.

Mule Deer's alert and horizontal ears betray the
blackened trees as dead and
herself as alive.
My steps snap the glittering fresh crust and then
push
into the soft undersnow. The snap and then the
laying down. I lift out for next step, snow ever
at each snowshoe hole.

Steel grey sky, to her slight body brings warmth.

Mule Deer person is so quiet I don't hear her, I look to the ridge as clouds open and close, breaking pieces of light onto the mountain. Her dark face lightens somewhat, a copper brown forehead and earth black nose.

Karol and I have been making love all fall and winter. We feel old to the game, to the romancing and the flattery, to the glance and the gasp. We are kind and generous with one another, expecting only forgiveness, giving it easily. Our white hairs and deep sleeps together are effortless.

Karol's dick, though, rises healthy and young and he presses his taut carpenter's torso to mine with intent. He rubs his greying beard on the tiny horizontal scar across my throat.

We smile a lot. It's as easy as walking in fresh snow.

The Majority of Which Falls as Snow

Only 5% of the rain and snow on Okanagan Mountain becomes groundwater. Tree people and plant people drink water, and the sky drinks back most of what it leaves for us. Only 13 mm a year—2%—of the rain and snow that falls here is taken by human people. 13 mm for coffee, wine, showers, soup, grass, grass, grass, grass, grass. If our grass takes more than 13 mm, from which people shall human people take water? Deer people? Pine people? Bear people?

"Annual precipitation over the Okanagan Basin averages approximately 554 mm, the majority of which falls as snow. Although precipitation for the period June—October averages 237 mm, most of it evaporates before it can runoff."

Breath, like water, finds a way. While travelling over the unnamed straight between island and mainland, and without anesthetizing my throat, the doctor slid a clean blade into my infant windpipe. A small amount of blood fell from the hole in my throat. The doctor carefully cleaned the skin around the hole. I was suddenly silent, my screams lost between lungs and mouth. My sudden silence frightened my mother, who thought I had died. But the doctor turned to her and said, "This silence indicates that your daughter's tracheotomy that I have just now performed on this boat has been a success. She may breathe thus through a tiny hole. As for the puzzle of burns on her body and arms, for now we should avoid touching them. When we arrive on the mainland we will take her to a hospital."

When Stresses Build up in the Earth like When an Elastic Band Is Stretched

"Earthquakes are a potential hazard in British Columbia. They are caused when stresses build up in the earth much like what happens when an elastic band is stretched. Eventually the earth's crust suddenly ruptures forming a fault, or a break in the crust, and instantaneously releasing the stored energy. The energy travels through the earth as waves similar to the waves produced by a pebble dropped into water. These waves are powerful and may cause widespread destruction."

Like an elastic band stretched out

Like an elastic band stretched

Like an elastic band

Like an elastic

Like Like Like Like Like the energy travels through water

Like the may cause and the suddenly ruptures

What If

What if I skies are also tired of dry forests, what if the clouds' favourite game is raining on fire, what if winds are in love with licking flames along treetops. Isn't a fire a great gift to sky?

A Very Bad Trail at That Time along the Mountainside

"The first record of a wagon train passing through the Okanagan Valley was when in 1858 the expedition of Palmer and Miller started out with nine wagons with supplies that would be needed by the gold miners from Walla-Walla, Wash., and after many hardships and adventures finally managed to reach Fort Kamlopps [sic] where they were able to sell all their goods and supplies and also the oxen and horses which hauled the loaded wagons. One of the highlights of this journey was the crossing of Okanagan Lake, from the vicinity of where Peachland now is, to the mouth of Mission Creek. Rafts were constructed, the wagons taken apart, and loaded onto the 50 rafts with all the supplies. The horses and oxen were driven back to Penticton, over the East side trail through Wild Horse Canyon—a very bad trail at that time along the mountainside. It was so bad that Father Pandosy with the help of his companions and Indians built a new trail by way of Chute Lake."

A very bad trail at that time along the mountainside

A very bad trail at that time along the

A very bad trail at that time along

A very bad trail at that time

A very bad trail at that

A very bad trail at

A very bad trail

A very bad

Priest Father Pandosy is a
priest at that time that at
priest is a Father Pandosy
fuck Father Pandosy

Drinking Water at Divide Lake

Along the cliff an angled ledge,
I climb down, lay on these little
cliff-pebbles, see the flat black water.

I fall my body down twenty
centimetres further and the
water is not still, I see these
clouds of eruptions, green
and glossy pulses.

Insects touch down, their
bodies pressing satellite
circles across the lake.

I tie an open water bottle to a
rope, lower the rope to the
water, watch the bottle slide
underwater as it fills. I pull my
body up, higher, and in my

eyes the lake stills, darkens
with distance. I add little blue
chlorine tablets to the

water, tighten the lid,
shake it and shake it.
Little pieces of sand and
wings float in the bottle.
I drink the unwilded water.

The Plane Struck a Tree

"This we know for certain: the plane struck a tree, turned slightly less than 180 degrees and came to rest facing away from its proper course. The cockpit had been sheared off, some of the seats in the cabin broke loose and slid forward with hand baggage and the passengers themselves. The plane lay shattered in three feet of snow on the east side of Okanagan Mountain at about 4500 feet."

The plane struck a tree

The plane lay in three feet of snow on the east side of Okanagan Mountain at about 4500 feet

"... [T]he dazed passengers had no idea where they were. Stewardess Lorna Franco asked: 'Is everybody all right?' A few passengers said they were bruised but okay. Others had blackened eyes: amazingly there were no broken bones."

Stewardess Lorna Franco asked: Is everybody all right?

A few passengers said they were bruised but okay.

Others had blackened eyes.

Amazingly.

"... aircraft did not catch fire due to (a) deep, wet snow on the ground and the presence of snow-laden trees and (b) due to the nature of the impact, fuel tanks were not fractured and the only escaping gasoline was from fractured fuel lines."

did not catch fire due to (a) deep,

wet

snow on the ground and the presence of snow

-laden trees and (b) due to the

nature of the impact, fuel tanks were not

fractured.

"One man reportedly reached for an axe to chop through the door."

confusion arose

reached through

"... [O]nce the survivors had been led down the trail on foot from the crash site and the bodies of the pilot and the co-pilot had been carried down from the mountain on toboggans, there were two additional efforts required to complete the story of the crash on Okanagan Mountain."

once the survivors

carried down from the

mountain

"... [O]nce everything of any value had been removed, the fuselage of the plane, the engines and the remaining debris burned to avoid any possibility of a future rescue effort mistaking the plane for a recent crash. Then there remained only the fuselage which lay on the mountain for several years until Jack Serwa of Kelowna salvaged it for an American firm that dealt in DC-3 parts."

everything of value had been

removed

then there remained only

"After that there remained only a scar in the trees and a trail leading in from the Chute Lake Road, mute testament to the crash and concerted effort of the determined people who put their hearts into the rescue. Only later, after it was all over, would the magnitude of the operation hit home to those involved."

after that there remained only *their hearts*

would *the magnitude of*

those involved *hit* *home*

"Because of the deaths of the pilot and co-pilot, the question of how the accident occurred has never been clearly answered. The subsequent reports and recommendations all skirted certain conclusions that could only have been made with first-hand testimony detailing what actually happened in the cockpit of Flight 4 in those last fatal seconds. Over a cloud-covered Okanagan Mountain the plane was supposed to have picked up the radio signal, which should have illuminated a small light on the instrument panel to tell Captain Moore that he was in line with the runway. At that instant he should have been high enough to clear the trees; but, as we know, he was not. Was there something wrong with his altimeter? This seems to be the most logical conclusion. Normal procedure calls for the pilots to re-set the altimeter periodically to make corrections for changes in air pressure. Were those adjustments not made that day? We will never know."

the question of how

never

certain conclusions

what actually illuminated

a small light

in line

clear the trees

he was not something wrong normal

corrections *changes* *corrections* *changes*

adjustments

adjustments *adjustments*

adjustments *adjustments*

adjustments

not made

we will know

In 1950 Ponderosa Pine People Bring Human People Home to Mountain

Ponderosa Pine people and Mountain were lonely for humans' small soft paws, dear flesh fingers rasping on bark, little breath cabinets opening into star skies.

Ponderosa Pine people heard a skybubble of human people breath, human people whisper, and Mountain sighed for it had been so long since people walked at night on Mountain.

Ponderosa Pine people reached their arms high above snow, scrabbled at airplane's heat ticket.

Ponderosa Pine brought human people home to Mountain for the solstice.

The Wreckage 70 Years Later

The 2020 photo of what is left of the wreckage, where pilot and co-pilot died, shows only two pieces of metal wreckage.

One piece of an engine and one piece of a wing.

Behind and around the pieces are coal and grey pieces of burned trees, thick berry brush, and no standing trees. Not a one. Not a pine. Not a spruce. Not a cottonwood.

One piece of a wing and one piece of an engine.

Only tangling sharp dark and grey and bone and coal branches and brushes and thorns. Not a tree for kilometres.

Of a wing, one piece, and of an engine, one piece.

Today this little plane would skim the mountain, not a branch to bristle the plane's wing, not a treetop to tickle, all normal flight at night.

In 1970 Plane Crash Passenger Dorothy Parker Recalls Some Details of the Pines

"Tree after tree fell as we ploughed on, making a swathing pathway through the forest... as if trying to pull us closer to earth."

as if

pull us closer

"But as we descended now we could clearly see the treetops being snipped off by the impact of our plane ploughing through the forest—like a giant lawnmower. The trees were below us, above us, beside us—as we made the desperate struggle to recover altitude."

like a below

us above us

beside as we

"A fleeting glance revealed that we were heading towards a giant pine tree, branches stretched menacingly upward—as if pointing to a highway in the sky. A thunderous crash followed as a wing slashed through the trunk and the tree, sheared and splintered, toppled sickeningly towards us, brushing the wings as it came to rest on the snow."

as if a highway

towards

us to rest on

snow

"With the help of the hatchet, slabs of tree trunks were hacked off and in the clearing in the snow, a small fire was coaxed along, and pungent black smoke began twisting towards the sky. For some crazy reason, we spread some blankets, obtained from the plane, on the snow near the fire. We sat down and half disappeared out of sight as we sank deep into the snow. One person, I recall, had an umbrella and only the top was left to mark her descent. It was the first time anyone had dared laugh."

off and in the

clearing

the snow

a small

fire

we spread

we sat

half disappeared

the first time

"The leading edges of the wing were nicked by the Jack pine whose trunk had been sliced through, and a bough was caught right in the shattered landing light."

whose trunk had been

sliced through

a bough

in the shattered

landing

light.

"Branches were ripped off the fir trees and the word 'DOC' was formed on a clearing so perchance, if a plane sighted us, this would warn him of our necessity for medical help."

ripped the

fir trees

and the word

sighted us

warn of our necessity

"We were to learn we were on a mountain towering above Chute Lake, 20 miles northeast of Penticton. The search plane flew level with the wreck to establish its altitude at 4,000 feet—about 1,000 feet below Mount Okanagan Peak."

mountain towering

flew level

peak

Story of Ponderosa Pine Seeking Fire for Pinecones and Space from Spruce

Another reason the trees may have reached for an airplane is that they were thirsty to burn.

Priest and logger's men put out fires for a century, dropping water from planes, spraying fire retardant on pine's high tops. Without fire, Engelmann Spruce and Black Cottonwood overtook more and more Ponderosa Pine forest. Cottonwood overleafed creeks all summer, Spruce crowded out pine saplings, and Ponderosa Pine's cones dried and decomposed, their seeds unreleased.

For a century, Ponderosa Pine looked for help from human people. Where were the humans who once burned fires at nights, who once slept months among the pine groves? Those human people who would let sparks birth more pine seedlings?

Who would release Cottonwood and Spruce people to ash, open ways for Berry people, Flower people, Bear people, Badger people?

Where were the young men and women who watched fires with love, with joy, with hand-over-flame caress?

1950 Solstice, the Ponderosa Pines, their vanilla bark chilled and dry, could smell the dark engine.

Firebirth! Sapboil! Coalblood!

But after so long, Ponderosa Pine wanted the firelove too much. Ponderosa Pine forgot how to burn well.

Treepeople pulled the plane into snow but were, alas, unable to burn. Ponderosa Pine had forgotten snow and fire's enmity.

This plane crash broke Ponderosa Pine's heart. The high cold snow cooled the plane's engines, and though fuel spilled from the plane, it could not ignite in the cold damp.

Mountain promised Ponderosa Pine people another fire, a summer fire.

Bark

Ponderosa Pine bark wraps a red

blood puzzle around cambium

heart. In hot sun, oldest bark resin

smells of vanilla. Bark grows outward,

thicker, piece by piece, ridges

between them deeper and

darker every year. These old bark-thick

Pine people are nearly fireproof, so that

after the summer fire of 2003, some very

old, very bark-thick Pine people still stood,

needles green against sooty trunks.

In an opposite way, the keloid

scars on my torso have become

softer and flatter for each decade I

grow away from my first bodyfire. As an

infant my burned body was first marked by

raised, red, scars. As I grew, my flat

girlchest became a raised scar map of

moraines, crags, flesh rivers seeping

around my arms. Tiny burn creases

radiated from my girl mouth, childwrinkles.

In time these hard scars softened, paled;

aging is an easy line away from that

trauma. After these decades of healing, the

scars barely rise from my papery old woman skin.

Experiential Entities Thus Perceive One Another

Karol and I drive to the mountain on a cold day, just as winter night recedes, coming to the trailhead in blue early light. We come to say goodbye.
The trail begins along the steep east side of Mountain. We look down to monstrous fenced villas and private beaches. We walk this eastern switchback for one kilometre and then cut up into shaded Mountain valleys. As we ascend the first valley wall we must pick our way through huge boulders, frozen over in blue and grey veins. Then we are in the quiet cold valley, surrounded by young paper birch trees. Icicles reach from leafless boughs, tracing a glassy form along chalky birch trunks. We walk faster now, trying to stay warm, ascending to half-burned, snow-heavy, Ponderosa Pine stands. I am too cold to talk to Karol. I have told him nothing of the plane crash, or of the bears, or of rattlesnakes and cougars. I will tell him another, warmer, day, when Mountain is a memory. I hear our breathing and a soft shattering as we step through crusted snow.

Why have I
wasted walks in Mountain being angry.
Why have I
slipped past these Ponderosa Pine people,
lost in my mutterings,
neither smelling nor seeing
the blazing snow in blue morning light,
not hearing Deer person's
snuffling of last year's dried berries.

Why have I forgotten gratitude,
ever,
in the mountains,
and still Mountain,
in her interminable gravity,
presses the bitterness from my spirit.

So that upon descent
my eyes open,
my nose widens,
my ears alight,
and it is almost too late.
My heart opens
only in time for the waves of tiny grasses and pebbles on the final steps.

Truth and

Just as a bad man should leave a good family, I am saying goodbye to Mountain in this anticolonial romance.

I have come to love Okanagan Mountain. I am in love with Mountain's deep gulches, dusty dry creekbeds, corpulent lichen-sprawled stones, middens of red fall leaves, goat bones and deer hair, grouse squawk and aspen groves.

I love Okanagan Mountain and I am not a Syilx person. My people came here as church-building, gold-hoarding, land-fencing colonizers. I give no truck to our claim.

The snap in my footstep is indigenous to mountains I've never walked.

And so my unpitiable heartbreak. While I think I love Okanagan Mountain in the before time, the ocean time, the after-ocean time, the snow-melt time, the goat bone time, the future-forest time, my love for Mountain is barely one exhale of Mountain lifetime. I am new, I come from violence, and I have no claim.

End

Acknowledgements

My writing, thinking, and walking for this book would not have happened without the love, support, and friendship of many people in my life. Some of these people are Karol Gabanowicz, Hugo Bowman, Finn Bowman, Heather Wheating, Mikara Pettman, Emma Lind, Natalie Chambers, Tara Scurr, Sasha Johnston, and Jake Kennedy. The conditions of my employment at Okanagan College allow me to have time for walking, writing and thinking, and I acknowledge the benefits of employment at a unionized workplace. Every worker should have these benefits. I thank Bob Cowan for his helpful procurement of historical writing about the 1950 plane crash on Okanagan Mountain. I have thought often of the survivors, and of the loved ones of the pilot and co-pilot who passed as a result of the crash. I hope they have found peace. At Caitlin Press, I have immense gratitude for the patience, enthusiasm, and kindness of Vici Johnstone and Sarah Corsie. I am still working on my understanding of the ongoing genocidal violence upon which the state known as canada is built. I am very grateful and have deep respect for the learning and kindness shared with me by Pamela Barnes, Grouse Barnes, Bill Cohen, Frank Marchand, Jacinda Mack, Bev Sellars, Kanahus Manuel, Arthur Manuel, and my sister Mara Pootlass. As a settler colonial person, I recognize and am angry about the violence inherent in my ancestors' colonial acts and I realize, every day, the many ways in which I continue to benefit from colonialism. Syilx land and waters should be returned to Syilx Okanagan people. There is no reconciliation without truth, and settler colonialists are still far from the truth about the effects of colonial land theft and genocide. Author proceeds from this book will be donated to the Syilx Language House, a grassroots non-profit charitable society that carries on the work of Indigenous language revitalization.

Notes & Sources

"Bear Forest": Van Tighem, Kevin. *Bears without Fear*. Rocky Mountain Books, Calgary, Alberta: 2013.

"Fire Paper Body": Stein, Gertrude. *Composition as Explanation*. Hogarth Press, London: 1926.

"Birth and Danger": Hanh, Thich Nhat. *How to Love*. Parallax Press, Berkeley: 2014.

"These Experiential Entities": Ellis, Peter. *Panpsychism: The Philosophy of the Sensuous Cosmos*. Iff Books, New York: 2011.

"The Majority of Which Falls as Snow" & "When Stresses Build up in the Earth like When an Elastic Band Is Stretched": Murray M Roed and John D Greenough, Eds. *Okanagan Geology: British Columbia*. Okanagan Geology Committee, 2014.

"A Very Bad Trail at That Time along the Mountainside": Watt, George M. "Transportation by Road and Trail in the Okanagan Valley," *OHS, The Twenty-seventh report of the Okanagan Historical Society*. 50 – 57.

"The Plane Struck a Tree": Shinnick, John Peter. "Plane Down in the Okanagan," *Forty Sixth Report of the Okanagan Historical Society*. Wayside Press, Vernon, BC: 1982. 9 – 19.

"In 1970 Plane Crash Passenger Dorothy Parker Recalls Some Details of the Pines": Furness, Dorothy Butler. "A Miracle at Christmas: December 22nd, 1950." *Fortieth Report of the Okanagan Historical Society*. Wayside Press, Vernon, BC: 1977. 84 – 93.

About the Author

Photo by Michał Gabanowicz

Norah Bowman, a settler-colonial writer originally from Texada Island, BC, is a professor of English Literature and Gender Studies at Okanagan College, on unceded Syilx territory (Kelowna, BC). Bowman has a PhD in English and film studies from the University of Alberta. Her co-authored book *Amplify: Graphic Narratives of Feminist Resistance* (2019) tells stories of feminist resistance and liberation movements worldwide, and her academic research focusses on unsettling colonial resource extraction. Bowman's poetry often reflects on human and non-human connections, including connections to place, water, plants, and animals.